Herbal Magic

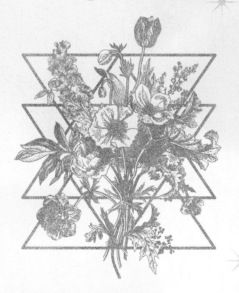

2024

WEEKLY PLANNER

JULY 2023 – DECEMBER 2024

ROCK POINT

2024 YEAR AT A GLANCE

JANUARY

S	M	T	W	T	F	S
	1	2	3	4	5	6
7	8	9	10	11	12	13
14	15	16	17	18	19	20
21	22	23	24	25	26	27
28	29	30	31			

FEBRUARY

S	M	T	W	T	F	S
				1	2	3
4	5	6	7	8	9	10
11	12	13	14	15	16	17
18	19	20	21	22	23	24
25	26	27	28	29		

MARCH

S	M	T	W	T	F	S
					1	2
3	4	5	6	7	8	9
10	11	12	13	14	15	16
17	18	19	20	21	22	23
24	25	26	27	28	29	30
31						

APRIL

S	M	T	W	T	F	S
	1	2	3	4	5	6
7	8	9	10	11	12	13
14	15	16	17	18	19	20
21	22	23	24	25	26	27
28	29	30				

MAY

S	M	T	W	T	F	S
			1	2	3	4
5	6	7	8	9	10	11
12	13	14	15	16	17	18
19	20	21	22	23	24	25
26	27	28	29	30	31	

JUNE

S	M	T	W	T	F	S
						1
2	3	4	5	6	7	8
9	10	11	12	13	14	15
16	17	18	19	20	21	22
23	24	25	26	27	28	29
30						

JULY

S	M	T	W	T	F	S
	1	2	3	4	5	6
7	8	9	10	11	12	13
14	15	16	17	18	19	20
21	22	23	24	25	26	27
28	29	30	31			

AUGUST

S	M	T	W	T	F	S
				1	2	3
4	5	6	7	8	9	10
11	12	13	14	15	16	17
18	19	20	21	22	23	24
25	26	27	28	29	30	31

SEPTEMBER

S	M	T	W	T	F	S
1	2	3	4	5	6	7
8	9	10	11	12	13	14
15	16	17	18	19	20	21
22	23	24	25	26	27	28
29	30					

OCTOBER

S	M	T	W	T	F	S
		1	2	3	4	5
6	7	8	9	10	11	12
13	14	15	16	17	18	19
20	21	22	23	24	25	26
27	28	29	30	31		

NOVEMBER

S	M	T	W	T	F	S
					1	2
3	4	5	6	7	8	9
10	11	12	13	14	15	16
17	18	19	20	21	22	23
24	25	26	27	28	29	30

DECEMBER

S	M	T	W	T	F	S
1	2	3	4	5	6	7
8	9	10	11	12	13	14
15	16	17	18	19	20	21
22	23	24	25	26	27	28
29	30	31				

2025 YEAR AT A GLANCE

JANUARY

S	M	T	W	T	F	S
			1	2	3	4
5	6	7	8	9	10	11
12	13	14	15	16	17	18
19	20	21	22	23	24	25
26	27	28	29	30	31	

FEBRUARY

S	M	T	W	T	F	S
						1
2	3	4	5	6	7	8
9	10	11	12	13	14	15
16	17	18	19	20	21	22
23	24	25	26	27	28	

MARCH

S	M	T	W	T	F	S
						1
2	3	4	5	6	7	8
9	10	11	12	13	14	15
16	17	18	19	20	21	22
23	24	25	26	27	28	29
30	31					

APRIL

S	M	T	W	T	F	S
		1	2	3	4	5
6	7	8	9	10	11	12
13	14	15	16	17	18	19
20	21	22	23	24	25	26
27	28	29	30			

MAY

S	M	T	W	T	F	S
				1	2	3
4	5	6	7	8	9	10
11	12	13	14	15	16	17
18	19	20	21	22	23	24
25	26	27	28	29	30	31

JUNE

S	M	T	W	T	F	S
1	2	3	4	5	6	7
8	9	10	11	12	13	14
15	16	17	18	19	20	21
22	23	24	25	26	27	28
29	30					

JULY

S	M	T	W	T	F	S
		1	2	3	4	5
6	7	8	9	10	11	12
13	14	15	16	17	18	19
20	21	22	23	24	25	26
27	28	29	30	31		

AUGUST

S	M	T	W	T	F	S
					1	2
3	4	5	6	7	8	9
10	11	12	13	14	15	16
17	18	19	20	21	22	23
24	25	26	27	28	29	30
31						

SEPTEMBER

S	M	T	W	T	F	S
	1	2	3	4	5	6
7	8	9	10	11	12	13
14	15	16	17	18	19	20
21	22	23	24	25	26	27
28	29	30				

OCTOBER

S	M	T	W	T	F	S
			1	2	3	4
5	6	7	8	9	10	11
12	13	14	15	16	17	18
19	20	21	22	23	24	25
26	27	28	29	30	31	

NOVEMBER

S	M	T	W	T	F	S
						1
2	3	4	5	6	7	8
9	10	11	12	13	14	15
16	17	18	19	20	21	22
23	24	25	26	27	28	29
30						

DECEMBER

S	M	T	W	T	F	S
	1	2	3	4	5	6
7	8	9	10	11	12	13
14	15	16	17	18	19	20
21	22	23	24	25	26	27
28	29	30	31			

BASIL | *Ocimum basilicum*

PLANETARY COMPANION	DAILY CORRESPONDENCE
MARS	TUESDAY
ZODIAC SIGN	ELEMENT
SCORPIO	FIRE
ENERGY	
MASCULINE	

The warming, slightly spicy flavor of basil makes it a favorite magical herb in the kitchen. In the language of herbs, basil offers good wishes. It's easy to grow indoors, if you do not have space outdoors. Let its sweet fragrance waft through your home, spreading a veil of protection from bad energies.

MAGICAL PROPERTIES
Basil's fresh scent stirs fidelity in love and opens the heart to forgiveness. Its mere presence in your pocket can invite wealth. Basil in the home guards against evil. It also offers protection and builds courage. Basil is revered for its divine essence.

SUGGESTED USE
Grow basil at each corner of your property, or hang sprigs in each of the four corners of your home, to create a barrier to evil influences. Infuse a tea for a special someone and invite love into your life, or add the tea to your ritual bath to increase your attractive energies. Give a basil plant as a housewarming gift to bestow good luck on the new home. Add to any love or money sachets.

Where basil leaves its scented trail, life's meant to be devoured. I call upon sweet basil's charm to heed my honest plea to garnish life with extra spice and increased spending power.

ENCHANTED BASIL BALSAMIC VINEGAR

Basil's magical properties are good for, among other things, fostering family love and boosting luck. This sweet, earthy vinegar is beautifully complemented by this aromatic herb. For more than just salads, dress grilled meats or vegetables, or dip in crusty bread for a peaceful family meal.

You will need:

- Two 28-ounce (828 ml) Mason jars with lids
- 1 cup (40 g) packed basil leaves, gently washed and thoroughly dried
- 2 cups (480 ml) balsamic vinegar
- Fine-mesh sieve and bowl to strain

1. Wash and dry the Mason jars.
2. Gently bruise or crush the basil to release the oils.
3. Place the basil in one jar, leaving 1 to 2 inches (2.5 to 5 cm) of space at the top.
4. Pour the vinegar over the basil, almost filling the jar.
5. Cover the jar with its lid and set aside in a cool, dark place for up to 2 weeks.

JULY 2023

NOTES	SUNDAY	MONDAY	TUESDAY
		2 ○	3	4
				INDEPENDENCE DAY (US)
	9 ◗	10	11
	16 ●	17	18
	23	24 ◖	25
	30	31	

JULY 2023

WEDNESDAY	THURSDAY	FRIDAY	SATURDAY
			1 CANADA DAY (CAN)
5	6	7	8
12	13	14	15
19	20	21	22
26	27	28	29

ELEMENTS

Nature's four key elements as revered by Western philosophies—fire, earth, air, and water—are found in the astrological Sun signs of the zodiac. Knowing the elemental correspondence of the herbs you're working with can enhance your herbal magic vocabulary and broaden the reach of the energies being transmitted into the Universe.

AIR: intellectual or spiritual capacity

EARTH: abundance, fertility, grounding, nourishing, sensuality

FIRE: banishing negativity, courage, protection, purification, sexuality

WATER: cleansing, nourishing, nurturing, soothing

JUNE / JULY

MONDAY (JUNE) 26

TUESDAY (JUNE) 27

WEDNESDAY (JUNE) 28

THURSDAY (JUNE) 29

FRIDAY (JUNE) 30

SATURDAY CANADA DAY (CAN) 1

SUNDAY 2

JULY 2023

MONDAY ○   **3**

TUESDAY INDEPENDENCE DAY (US)   **4**

WEDNESDAY   **5**

THURSDAY   **6**

FRIDAY 7

SATURDAY 8

SUNDAY 9

Protective potion, heed my plea, whose
spicy scented help I seek.
Do cloak me in your healing charms.
Protect me from life's many harms.

JULY 2023

MONDAY ◗   10

TUESDAY   11

WEDNESDAY   12

THURSDAY   13

FRIDAY 14

SATURDAY 15

SUNDAY 16

To clear the mind and cleanse the face,
I call on water's soothing grace.

JULY 2023

MONDAY ● 17

TUESDAY 18

WEDNESDAY 19

THURSDAY 20

FRIDAY 21

SATURDAY 22

SUNDAY 23

*Sit under a tree's welcoming branches
to ease stress and calm a harried heart.*

JULY 2023

MONDAY 24

TUESDAY 25

WEDNESDAY 26

THURSDAY 27

FRIDAY 28

SATURDAY 29

SUNDAY 30

Sprig of mint, dash of cloves,
basil leaf, and nutmeg whole,
season well my resume that fruitful
interviews come my way.

MUGWORT | *Artemisia vulgaris*

PLANETARY COMPANION	DAILY CORRESPONDENCE
VENUS	FRIDAY
ZODIAC SIGN	ELEMENT
PISCES	EARTH
ENERGY	
FEMININE	

Mugwort's name is said to relate to its favored use to flavor drinks, especially beer, before the more traditional hops entered the picture. Mugwort's language is one of happiness.

MAGICAL PROPERTIES
Mugwort is a powerful herbal ally, believed to offer strength, protection from evil, healing energies, amplification of other magic, increased intuition and wisdom, and clarity of observation. Associated with John the Baptist, who is said to have worn a band of mugwort during his time in the desert, it became known as the herb that could drive away demons.

SUGGESTED USE
Add the leaves to dream pillows when prophetic dreams are desired. Add the leaves to a warm bath to increase intuition and before meditation, scrying, or divination work. Tuck some into your shoes or a pocket on long journeys to keep up your strength and relieve jet lag at the end of travel. Hang from windows or doorways to prevent evil from entering your home. Safely burn instead of sage for smudging needs.

When cats do cry and birds do fly and
blackened clouds do fill the sky.
I light this herb to clear the air that only those who enter here
bring peace and joy and soothing way,
and evil fast and far does fly.

HECATE PROTECTION INCENSE

Hecate, the Queen of Witches, is the protector of the home. This spell calls on the powerful energy Hecate offers to protect and guide you. With your mortar and pestle, grind bay leaves, rose petals, lavender, and mugwort.

Once fully mixed, add essential oils:

- Rose
- Frankincense
- Lavender

Hold your hands over the mixture and say quietly or aloud:

Mother Hecate, on this dark moon I call to you.

With this smoke, I invite your energy.

Protect and guide me. Blessed be!

AUGUST 2023

NOTES	SUNDAY	MONDAY	TUESDAY
			○ 1
	6	7	☽ 8
		SUMMER BANK HOLIDAY (UK-SCT)	
	13	14	15
	20	21	22
	27	28	29
		SUMMER BANK HOLIDAY (UK-ENG / NIR / WAL)	

AUGUST 2023

WEDNESDAY	THURSDAY	FRIDAY	SATURDAY
2	3	4	5
9	10	11	12
16	17	18	19
23	24	25	26
30	31		

PLANT INTELLIGENCE

Defining "intelligence" related to plants is tricky and said to be measured based on memory and movement, adaptability, sensory abilities, and communication systems—not to mention growth and development—all reasons that can be argued for, and against, a plant's ability to possess and demonstrate intelligence.

Scientists today are beginning to understand that plants have an intelligence and ability to learn, remember, communicate, and cooperate. In a forest, trees exchange nutrients and information about threats and predators via an underground network of roots and fungi. Above ground, plants communicate using chemicals and scents to send warnings of danger, deter predators, and invite pollinating insects. Studies have shown that plants respond to sound, specifically a noise made between 125 Hz and 250 Hz, like that produced by running water.

And finally, yes, talking to your plants does seem to help them grow. So, between the vibrations of your aura, your voice, your thoughts, and your movements, your plants do look forward to your visits.

JULY / AUGUST

MONDAY (JULY) **31**

TUESDAY ○ **1**

WEDNESDAY **2**

THURSDAY **3**

FRIDAY **4**

SATURDAY **5**

SUNDAY **6**

AUGUST 2023

MONDAY SUMMER BANK HOLIDAY (UK-SCT)   **7**

TUESDAY ◗   **8**

WEDNESDAY   **9**

THURSDAY   **10**

FRIDAY **11**

SATURDAY **12**

SUNDAY **13**

Rowan's forces for good can counter negative energies—place a branch in the house, or wear a sprig for protection on the go.

AUGUST 2023

MONDAY 14

TUESDAY 15

WEDNESDAY ● ✳ 16

THURSDAY 17

FRIDAY 18

SATURDAY 19

SUNDAY 20

*Unleash your rich fragrance
into the world that my world
becomes richer for it.*

AUGUST 2023

MONDAY 21

TUESDAY 22

WEDNESDAY 23

THURSDAY 24

FRIDAY 25

SATURDAY 26

SUNDAY 27

When spirits sag and energies wane
a friend's embrace can oft sustain.

FRANKINCENSE | *Boswellia sacra / Boswellia carterii*

PLANETARY COMPANION	DAILY CORRESPONDENCE
SUN	**SUNDAY**
ZODIAC SIGN	ELEMENT
AQUARIUS	**FIRE**
ENERGY	
MASCULINE	

Among the three gifts given to honor the newborn baby Jesus, frankincense speaks of reverence and honor. It has a long history of ceremonial, spiritual, and healing uses and was once more valuable than the gold also given to honor Jesus. *Boswellia sacra* has been labeled "near threatened," and the species in general may be threatened due to habitat loss and overharvesting.

MAGICAL PROPERTIES
Incorporate frankincense responsibly into your herbal magic to call for protection, banish the unwanted and unhelpful, and open your heart and mind to spiritual work.

SUGGESTED USE
Burn as an incense to aid meditation and bring about a sense of grounding and perspective when the world seems to be spinning beyond your control. Smudge with frankincense to clear a space of negative energies and create space for spiritual work. Keep frankincense on your altar for protection.

From wise men once an honored gift, so valued are your ways.
Burn frankincense to cleanse the air and usher out the haze
that spirit guides may whisper wise and
healing words this day.

MERCURY RETROGRADE POTION

When Mercury, the planet of clarity and community, goes retrograde, everything seems to go wrong. This oil-potion will help protect you from the negative influences of Mercury retrograde and can be used to anoint candles, diffuse into the air, or wear dabbed on your throat and sacral chakras.

In a cleansed jar add frankincense, sweet orange, and ylang-ylang essential oils. Sprinkle in dried sage and orange peels.

Sit quietly in a dark, comfortable space and conjure images of clear and concise communication, no confusion, and the ability to move with dignity and grace.

O' Mercury, god of clarity, messenger to the gods,

I call on thee, retrograde free, to help me beat these odds.

Through my door, with spirits high, I banish all confusion,

and shield my soul, my spirit whole, from negative intrusion.

SEPTEMBER 2023

NOTES	SUNDAY	MONDAY	TUESDAY
	3	4	5
	FATHER'S DAY (AUS / NZ)	LABOR DAY (US) LABOUR DAY (CAN)	
	10	11	12
	GRANDPARENTS' DAY (US)	PATRIOT DAY (US)	
	17	18	19
	24	25	26
	YOM KIPPUR (BEGINS AT SUNDOWN)		

SEPTEMBER 2023

WEDNESDAY	THURSDAY	FRIDAY	SATURDAY
		1	2
6	7	8	9
13	14	15 ROSH HASHANAH (BEGINS AT SUNDOWN) FIRST DAY OF NATIONAL HISPANIC HERITAGE MONTH	16
20	21	22	23 FALL EQUINOX
27	28	29 SUKKOT (BEGINS AT SUNDOWN)	30

HERBAL MAGIC GUIDELINES

When using herbs to conjure magic in our lives, there are no rules except do no harm—to yourself, others, or Mother Earth—and know your plants. Without the millennia-long history of herbal healing, modern medicine might not exist today. And, while many of the herbs and flowers are culinary in nature, nothing should be consumed without first knowing its true properties and identification.

Some tips for herbal magic success:

- Be respectful, sustainable, and intentional in your herb growth, selection, harvesting, and use.

- Be respectful of your intuition; let it guide your herbal magic practice and relationship with the Universe.

- Work with the seasons to honor Nature's pace—perfection can't be hurried.

- Honor the herbs and plants you harvest and use them with gratitude for the energies offered.

AUGUST/SEPTEMBER

MONDAY (AUGUST) SUMMER BANK HOLIDAY (UK-ENG / NIR / WAL)   **28**

TUESDAY (AUGUST)   **29**

WEDNESDAY (AUGUST) ○   **30**

THURSDAY (AUGUST)   **31**

FRIDAY   **1**

SATURDAY   **2**

SUNDAY FATHER'S DAY (AUS / NZ)   **3**

SEPTEMBER 2023

MONDAY LABOR DAY (US) / LABOUR DAY (CAN) 4

TUESDAY 5

WEDNESDAY ☽ 6

THURSDAY 7

FRIDAY

8

SATURDAY

9

SUNDAY GRANDPARENTS' DAY (US)

10

With ivy crown and silken gown and veil of pure intent, my pledge today will never stray beyond our covenant.

SEPTEMBER 2023

MONDAY PATRIOT DAY (US)   **11**

TUESDAY   **12**

WEDNESDAY   **13**

THURSDAY ●   **14**

FRIDAY ROSH HASHANAH (BEGINS AT SUNDOWN) / FIRST DAY OF NATIONAL HISPANIC HERITAGE MONTH **15**

SATURDAY **16**

SUNDAY **17**

Sweet herbs and blooms whose charms doth soothe, do fill me with your calming voice to take up anger's place.

SEPTEMBER 2023

MONDAY 18

TUESDAY 19

WEDNESDAY 20

THURSDAY 21

FRIDAY ☽ **22**

SATURDAY FALL EQUINOX **23**

SUNDAY YOM KIPPUR (BEGINS AT SUNDOWN) **24**

With healing herbs I bless this space
with air so pure and healing grace.

DILL | *Anethum graveolens*

PLANETARY COMPANIONS	DAILY CORRESPONDENCES
MERCURY, JUPITER	WEDNESDAY, THURSDAY

ZODIAC SIGNS	ELEMENT
GEMINI, LEO, VIRGO	FIRE

ENERGY	
MASCULINE	

Love is in the air when dill is in the house. It softly whispers spicy words of lust. Turn on the kitchen magic anytime you season food with dill. It is also a vigorous grower and prolific self-seeder, indicating powers of fertility.

MAGICAL PROPERTIES
Attract love and romance (and a little lust) with dill's fresh scent, which can also bring you back into emotional and mental balance when times are not so heady. Dill attracts abundance and dispels negative energies. It is particularly useful in keeping the heart and mind balanced and in the moment.

SUGGESTED USE
Add a few sprigs to love potions, cocktails, or any beverage of choice to turn on the love charm. Line windowsills to keep out negative energy. Sprinkle on foods to charm your guests, or on your altar for good luck. Add seeds to charm bags for love spells. This airy plant just makes you feel good . . . sow some seeds where you can as you sow your intentions along with them and watch what happens.

There is no time to dilly-dally; it's love I seek today.
With seed, and leaf, and root of dill, I hungrily do pray
that romance and its courting dance do hurry here my way.

HERBAL FAVORS

Preserved herbs are the perfect DIY gifts with a special sentiment for friends and family. They can be used as tabletop decorations, as buffet garnishes, as ingredients in foods or cocktails. If it's around the holidays, add a looped ribbon to make the perfect ornament for the Christmas tree.

Place your chosen herb, or herbs, in a potpourri bag or a glass container in a shape that suits the occasion. Include a tag for instructions or a lovely description.

In the language of herbs, consider:

- Fern, for fascination
- Dill, for good spirits
- Mint, for warm feelings
- Myrtle, for love

OCTOBER 2023

NOTES	SUNDAY	MONDAY	TUESDAY
		1	2
			LABOUR DAY (AUS-ACT / NSW / SA)
	8	9	10
		INDIGENOUS PEOPLES' DAY (US) COLUMBUS DAY (US) THANKSGIVING DAY (CAN)	
	15	16	17
	22	23	24
		LABOUR DAY (NZ)	
	29	30	31
			HALLOWEEN

OCTOBER 2023

WEDNESDAY	THURSDAY	FRIDAY	SATURDAY
4	5 ☽	6	7 SIMCHAT TORAH (BEGINS AT SUNDOWN)
11	12	13 ●	14
18	19	20 ☾	21
25	26	27 ○	28

MEDITATION BASICS

Time in Nature has been proven to ease stress, boost creativity, increase focus, and promote empathy—valuable life tools, indeed. Adding meditation to enhance your herbal magic offers another tool to tap into your inner thoughts and feelings that can then become intentions set and energy released to achieve goals.

- Find a quiet, comfortable place, outside, if possible, to connect with the natural energies around, and that's ideal for boosting mood and peacefulness. Relax. Set a gentle alarm, if you want to time your session.

- Imagine your inhale has the scent of roses, or your favorite flower or herb, filling you from top to bottom, cleansing and clearing any negativity, hurt, or fear.

- Visualize your exhale, taking with it anything causing you pain as you replace it on the inhale with soothing kindness.

- Focus. Keep your attention on your breath. When it wanders, gently acknowledge it and return your focus to your breath.

SEPTEMBER/OCTOBER

MONDAY (SEPTEMBER) — 25

TUESDAY (SEPTEMBER) — 26

WEDNESDAY (SEPTEMBER) — 27

THURSDAY (SEPTEMBER) — 28

FRIDAY (SEPTEMBER) SUKKOT (BEGINS AT SUNDOWN) ○ — 29

SATURDAY (SEPTEMBER) — 30

SUNDAY — 1

OCTOBER 2023

MONDAY LABOUR DAY (AUS-ACT / NSW / SA)   **2**

TUESDAY   **3**

WEDNESDAY   **4**

THURSDAY   **5**

FRIDAY ◗ 6

SATURDAY SIMCHAT TORAH (BEGINS AT SUNDOWN) 7

SUNDAY 8

*Recharging herbs are strewn anew
to boost energies and keep us safe.*

OCTOBER 2023

MONDAY INDIGENOUS PEOPLES' DAY (US) / COLUMBUS DAY (US) / THANKSGIVING DAY (CAN)   9

TUESDAY   10

WEDNESDAY   11

THURSDAY   12

FRIDAY 13

SATURDAY 14

SUNDAY 15

Your stems stand strong to urge me on,
to stand and face the fray.

OCTOBER 2023

MONDAY 16

TUESDAY 17

WEDNESDAY 18

THURSDAY 19

FRIDAY   20

SATURDAY   21

SUNDAY   22

Accept who you are. Talk to yourself
as you would your best friend.

OCTOBER 2023

MONDAY LABOUR DAY (NZ) 23

TUESDAY 24

WEDNESDAY 25

THURSDAY 26

FRIDAY 27

SATURDAY ○ 28

SUNDAY 29

*Herbs of courage do fill my heart
with strength to do and will to start.*

SANDALWOOD (AUSTRALIAN) | *Santalum spicatum*
SANDALWOOD (HAWAIIAN) | *Santalum paniculatum*
SANDALWOOD (INDIAN; ENDANGERED) | *Santalum album*

PLANETARY COMPANION	DAILY CORRESPONDENCE
MOON	MONDAY
ZODIAC SIGNS	ELEMENT
CANCER, LEO	WATER
ENERGY	
FEMININE	

With its long history of ritual use and sweet, spicy aroma, sandalwood is said to scent the heavens as a favorite fragrance of the gods. On Earth, Indian sandalwood is a threatened species and should be respected as such. Vintage sandalwood items, such as prayer beads, can be sourced and used responsibly. Australian and Hawaiian varieties of sandalwood are grown now as options.

MAGICAL PROPERTIES
Sandalwood is calming, which is useful in meditative work; seek sandalwood for granting of wishes, peace of mind, purification, safety, and trust.

SUGGESTED USE
Often used as an incense and in aromatherapy blends, sandalwood mixed with lavender helps you work with the angels; when mixed with jasmine, it can induce soothing dreams. Write your wishes on a piece of paper and safely burn it over a sandalwood-scented candle, or with sandalwood incense, and await the response as your wishes are carried to the Universe on the sweet-smelling smoke.

With sandalwood and candles three,
I light your flames with prayer to free
my wishes into space, where they'll swiftly manifest and come to me.

SAFE & SOUND OIL

Dabbing on your throat and sacral chakras, as well as on your wrists, before starting your day is suggested for the best results.
Gather these items:

- 3 slightly crushed, whole black peppercorns
- 10 drops of each essential oil:
  - Geranium
  - Neroli
  - Lemon
  - Sandalwood
  - Frankincense

Fill your glass receptacle with your carrier oil, leaving about 1 to 2 inches (2.5 to 5 cm) of space at the top. Add each ingredient while visualizing negativity bouncing off of your spiritual umbrella like rain and say:

O' sacred pepper, I call on you to keep me safe and sound.

Banish evil spirits and bring blessings that abound.

Soteria, infuse this potion with all your godly charm,

so all who use it to anoint will surely evade harm.

NOVEMBER 2023

NOTES	SUNDAY	MONDAY	TUESDAY
	5	6	7
			ELECTION DAY (US)
	12	13	14
	FIRST DAY OF DIWALI		
	19	20	21
	26	27	28

NOVEMBER 2023

WEDNESDAY	THURSDAY	FRIDAY	SATURDAY
1 ALL SAINTS' DAY	2	3	4
8	9	10	11 VETERANS DAY (US)
15	16	17	18
22	23 THANKSGIVING DAY (US)	24 NATIVE AMERICAN HERITAGE DAY (US)	25
29	30		

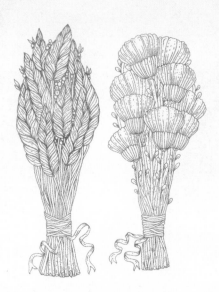

GATHERING YOUR MAGICAL HERBAL BOUNTY

Whether snipping and pruning herbs in your own garden, from pots, or from the grocery store or farmers' market, begin with gratitude. Honor the bounty brought forth from the Earth for the pure magical delight that it is and for the energy, nourishment, and magic it lends to your life. When you can, replant what you harvest—whether with the same or something new—to continue the cycle.

Harvest:

- Harvesting herbs: Pick herb leaves before flowers develop on the plants; gather herbs on warm mornings, after their awakening kiss of dew has evaporated.

- Harvesting flowers: Snip newly emerged blossoms from the plants a day or two after they've bloomed.

- Harvesting seeds: The herbs' flavorful and potent energies live on in the plants' seeds. Harvest the seed heads when they are mostly brown and hardening but not yet burst, with as long of a stem attached as you can.

OCTOBER / NOVEMBER

MONDAY (OCTOBER)   30

TUESDAY (OCTOBER) HALLOWEEN   31

WEDNESDAY ALL SAINTS' DAY   1

THURSDAY   2

FRIDAY   3

SATURDAY   4

SUNDAY   5

November 2023

MONDAY 6

TUESDAY ELECTION DAY (US) 7

WEDNESDAY 8

THURSDAY 9

FRIDAY 10

SATURDAY VETERANS DAY (US) 11

SUNDAY FIRST DAY OF DIWALI 12

With lady's mantle dew so rare,
upon my face that I do dare believe
its beauty will outshine, all those
who seek my lover's time.

NOVEMBER 2023

MONDAY ● 13

TUESDAY 14

WEDNESDAY 15

THURSDAY 16

FRIDAY 17

SATURDAY 18

SUNDAY 19

When stars align and herbs do shine,
the love I seek is truly mine.

NOVEMBER 2023

MONDAY ◖ **20**

TUESDAY **21**

WEDNESDAY **22**

THURSDAY THANKSGIVING DAY (US) **23**

FRIDAY NATIVE AMERICAN HERITAGE DAY (US)

24

SATURDAY

25

SUNDAY

26

With violet posy tucked close by,
a wish for all my friends,
the faithful friendships that we
yearn to last until the end.

CINNAMON (CEYLON) | *Cinnamomum verum* or *Cinnamomum zeylanicum*

PLANETARY COMPANIONS
SUN, JUPITER

DAILY CORRESPONDENCES
SUNDAY, THURSDAY

ZODIAC SIGN
AQUARIUS

ELEMENT
FIRE

ENERGY
MASCULINE

Ceylon cinnamon, or true cinnamon, is native to Sri Lanka, and has a delicate sweet taste. A symbol of status in the ancient world, cinnamon, in the language of flowers, is one of generosity—what's mine is yours. A warming culinary spice, it brings feelings of comfort, coziness, love, and safety.

MAGICAL PROPERTIES
Cinnamon increases spirituality; breeds abundance, power, and success; inspires love and lust; and offers protection.

SUGGESTED USE
With its association to fire, add cinnamon to any spell to help it manifest more quickly. Cinnamon in potpourri is a lovely way to add soothing fragrance and its magical energies to a room. Hang a cinnamon broom over the main doorway to your home for protective energy; liberally season foods with cinnamon and taste what success is like. Burn cinnamon incense to ignite romance. Sprinkle a dollar bill with cinnamon, fold it five times while imagining your newfound wealth, and put it in your wallet.

With sprinkle, dash, a pinch or two of secret
spice of tannish hue
I hereby cast out evil harm and do invoke protective charm.

SPICE OF CONFIDENCE

When that nagging voice in your head is wearing you down, it's time to act to still the voice and conjure confidence. Call on the power of the Sun and any number of Sun-correspondence herbs, such as black tea, chamomile, cinnamon, frankincense, ginseng, orange blossom, rosemary, or turmeric.

Each and every herb created by Nature is a perfect living thing—just like you. Each and every herb has its perfect traits and talents—just like you. Each and every herb will in turn boost another just by its existence—just like you. Nature is beautiful and perfect—just like you.

O' brilliant Sun, whose energy does urge these herbs to grow,

illuminate the confidence within my heart to know

that who I am is perfect—as above, so below.

DECEMBER 2023

NOTES	SUNDAY	MONDAY	TUESDAY
	3	**4**	**5**
	INTERNATIONAL DAY OF PERSONS WITH DISABILITIES		
	10	**11**	**12**
	HUMAN RIGHTS DAY		
	17	**18**	**19**
	24	**25**	**26**
	CHRISTMAS EVE		BOXING DAY (UK / CAN / AUS / NZ)
	31		
	NEW YEAR'S EVE	CHRISTMAS DAY	FIRST DAY OF KWANZAA

DECEMBER 2023

WEDNESDAY	THURSDAY	FRIDAY	SATURDAY
		1 WORLD AIDS DAY	2
6	7 HANUKKAH (BEGINS AT SUNDOWN)	8	9
13	14	15	16
20	21 WINTER SOLSTICE	22	23
27	28	29	30

STORING DRIED HERBS

Storing herbs properly preserves their culinary and magical properties longer, and honors the work you've done in harmony with Nature to tend and nurture your herbs to maturity. Protecting them from moisture, sunlight, and air is key.

Remove the dried leaves from the stems, discarding the stems. You can store the leaves whole or crumble them, as you wish, but whole herbs last longer. Remove the seeds from the seed heads or pods. You may want to work over a sheet pan or parchment paper to catch the leaves and seeds as they fall. Remove husks from seeds, as needed, by gently rubbing the seeds between your hands.

Store the leaves, seeds, or flowers separately, in airtight containers in a cool, dark place to preserve their aroma and color. They will keep for 6 to 12 months.

NOVEMBER/DECEMBER

MONDAY (NOVEMBER) ○   27

TUESDAY (NOVEMBER)   28

WEDNESDAY (NOVEMBER)   29

THURSDAY (NOVEMBER)   30

FRIDAY WORLD AIDS DAY   1

SATURDAY   2

SUNDAY INTERNATIONAL DAY OF PERSONS WITH DISABILITIES   3

DECEMBER 2023

MONDAY   4

TUESDAY   5

WEDNESDAY   6

THURSDAY HANUKKAH (BEGINS AT SUNDOWN)   7

FRIDAY 8

SATURDAY 9

SUNDAY HUMAN RIGHTS DAY 10

When lacking courage to face the day,
I call on thyme to ease my way.

DECEMBER 2023

MONDAY 11

TUESDAY 12

WEDNESDAY 13

THURSDAY 14

FRIDAY 15

SATURDAY 16

SUNDAY 17

Of mint or lime and chocolate, too, sweet geranium's scents my stress undo.

DECEMBER 2023

MONDAY   18

TUESDAY   19

WEDNESDAY   20

THURSDAY WINTER SOLSTICE   21

FRIDAY 22

SATURDAY 23

SUNDAY CHRISTMAS EVE 24

Cleopatra is said to have considered aloe vital to her beauty routine.

DECEMBER 2023

MONDAY CHRISTMAS DAY   **25**

TUESDAY BOXING DAY (UK / CAN / AUS / NZ) / FIRST DAY OF KWANZAA ○   **26**

WEDNESDAY   **27**

THURSDAY   **28**

FRIDAY 29

SATURDAY 30

SUNDAY NEW YEAR'S EVE 31

To tackle dust and dirt and grime,
your mighty scent does shine.
To cleanse, protect, and heal my
home, I turn at once to pine.

NUTMEG | *Myristica fragrans*

PLANETARY COMPANION	DAILY CORRESPONDENCE
JUPITER	THURSDAY
ZODIAC SIGNS	ELEMENT
PISCES, SAGITTARIUS	FIRE
ENERGY	
MASCULINE	

This beloved spice, often associated with the winter holidays, is a cozy, warming herb. Its message is of invitation—especially to a meeting; you decide whether for business or pleasure.

MAGICAL PROPERTIES

Nutmeg is the best at attracting money and luck—and luck with money when gambling—as well as love. Nutmeg's warming qualities can also be soothing.

SUGGESTED USE

Sprinkle nutmeg in a glass of warm milk or chamomile tea and sip before bed to slip comfortably into dreamland. Carry a whole nutmeg for luck, but especially to spice up your odds of winning in any game of chance, or regarding legal matters pending a decision. Sprinkle ground nutmeg into money charms or over your altar for money spells, or use nutmeg essential oil to anoint candles for the same. Sharing a nutmeg-garnished food or beverage with someone special is said to stir up love—especially in front of a roaring fire.

For craps or slots, and poker, too, rub lucky nutmeg in my shoe.
When carried, worn, and sprinkled on, this spicy herb turns on the charm
if dice are cold and slots don't hit, it's nutmeg's chance to work the pit
to turn your luck from cold to hot and guarantee you'll cry, "Jackpot!"

A GAMBLER'S LUCK

It's true . . . you need to know when to fold 'em, but before calling it quits, call Lady Luck to your side and take her for a spin. Particularly lucky herbs to take along for the ride include acorn, basil, coriander, mint, borage, bachelor's button, nutmeg, rosemary, and poppy.

This herbal brew I offer you in hopes you'll cheer me on . . .

with lucky glances and improved chances bolstering my courage,

so, deal away, luck's here to play; the pot is growing strong.

JANUARY 2024

NOTES	SUNDAY	MONDAY	TUESDAY
		1 NEW YEAR'S DAY	2 NEW YEAR HOLIDAY (UK-SCT)
	7	8	9
	14	15 CIVIL RIGHTS DAY (US) MARTIN LUTHER KING JR. DAY (US)	16
	21	22	23
	28	29	30

JANUARY 2024

WEDNESDAY	THURSDAY	FRIDAY	SATURDAY
☾ 3	4	5	6
10	● 11	12	13
☾ 17	18	19	20
24	○ 25	26 AUSTRALIA DAY (AUS)	27 HOLOCAUST REMEMBRANCE DAY
31			

MANY SAFE RETURNS

Make a simple travel spell bag to tuck into your luggage, purse, pocket, or glove compartment to ensure a safe return home.

For Protection	For Calm	For Jet Lag
Acorn	Chamomile	Gentian
Angelica	Frankincense	Ginseng
Basil	Lavender	Mugwort
Comfrey	Lemon balm	Passionflower

Fold them into a bundle, and tie it tightly with a white ribbon, the color of spiritual purity. Feel gratitude for the protection afforded by the herbs. Say quietly or aloud:

With herbs tucked safely in this bag,
they'll see my journey has no lag.
That safely I return to home.
each time life calls for me to roam.

JANUARY

MONDAY NEW YEAR'S DAY | 1

TUESDAY NEW YEAR HOLIDAY (UK-SCT) | 2

WEDNESDAY ☽ | 3

THURSDAY | 4

FRIDAY | 5

SATURDAY | 6

SUNDAY | 7

JANUARY 2024

MONDAY 8

TUESDAY 9

WEDNESDAY 10

THURSDAY ● 11

FRIDAY   12

SATURDAY   13

SUNDAY   14

*This warming cup is just the stuff
to keep the germs at bay.*

JANUARY 2024

MONDAY CIVIL RIGHTS DAY (US) / MARTIN LUTHER KING JR. DAY (US)   15

TUESDAY   16

WEDNESDAY   17

THURSDAY   18

FRIDAY 19

SATURDAY 20

SUNDAY 21

Bleeding heart can open your heart to unconditional love after loss and ease the pain of a broken heart.

JANUARY 2024

MONDAY   22

TUESDAY   23

WEDNESDAY   24

THURSDAY ○   25

FRIDAY AUSTRALIA DAY (AUS)

26

SATURDAY HOLOCAUST REMEMBRANCE DAY

27

SUNDAY

28

O' bloom whose charms do so delight,
I seek your counsel wise, do tell of love
or fond delight within my lover's eyes.

VIOLA | *Viola* spp.

PLANETARY COMPANIONS	DAILY CORRESPONDENCE
SATURN, VENUS	SATURDAY
ZODIAC SIGNS	ELEMENT
LIBRA, SAGITTARIUS, TAURUS	WATER
ENERGY	
FEMININE	

Viola's sweet bloom is among the first in spring, when her cheerful face is like a balm to our winter souls. Viola, though delicate in appearance, is might in persistence, taking up residence throughout your garden patch before you even know it. Her language of flowers speaks of faithfulness, and she will return each spring with her messages of love. Because of her ability to reseed so well, viola is also associated with rebirth.

MAGICAL PROPERTIES
Viola is a faithful companion in loving charm, inducing tender thoughts and luck in love. She promotes thoughtfulness, patience, protection, and wishes granted.

SUGGESTED USE
Toss in a salad or garnish an iced drink. Add a drop of violet liqueur to scones or shortbread for a floral lift. Mix into a cocktail, if you dare, to send vibrations of love, or infuse into a tea. Violas tucked into a posy can be filled with your intentions and given as gifts to bring love, luck, and protection. Candied violas are a favorite of garden fairies and make lovely decorations on baked goods. A simple bunch on your altar can imbue your magical practice with loving thoughts and intentions manifested.

Sweet viola, whose face does enchant, turn your lovely gaze my way
that no harm befalls kith or kin as you stand
watch from your garden's glen.

MOONLIT GROUNDING

Grounding is the act of placing your bare feet on a natural surface—sand, soil, grass, or mud—to create a connection between your body and the Earth's energy or natural charge. This can be particularly powerful during the Waxing Moon.

1. Find a peaceful place outside where the Moon is visible with a surface that is easy on your feet.

2. Stand with your bare feet on the Earth. Close your eyes and breathe slowly. Wiggle your toes and shift your weight until your feet settle into a deep and comfortable connection with the ground.

3. Stay in this position for 5 minutes. Think about any challenges or obstacles you've been facing.

4. Open your eyes and slowly walk barefoot in a large circle. Take your steps gently, but with intention. Notice the way each bare foot connects with the Earth. Notice your posture.

5. Walk this way for a few minutes. You may find that you feel charged by the Earth and have increased clarity when connecting with yourself, identifying the action you want to take, or addressing the challenges you may be facing.

FEBRUARY 2024

NOTES	SUNDAY	MONDAY	TUESDAY
	4	5	6 WAITANGI DAY OBSERVED (NZ)
	11	12	13
	18	19 PRESIDENTS' DAY (US)	20
	25	26	27

FEBRUARY 2024

WEDNESDAY	THURSDAY	FRIDAY	SATURDAY
	1	2	3
	FIRST DAY OF BLACK HISTORY MONTH	GROUNDHOG DAY (US / CAN)	
7	8	9	10
			CHINESE NEW YEAR
14	15	16	17
VALENTINE'S DAY ASH WEDNESDAY			
21	22	23	24
28	29		

DEMETER/CERES

Demeter (Ceres was her Roman name) was the Greek goddess of agriculture/food, plants, and law and order, arising from the transition to an agrarian society with defined living and planting areas. Ceres lends her name to cereal, meaning cultivated grain, and is sought for her powers of abundance, fertility, and endurance. Sacred plants to her were the chaste tree, corn, and pumpkin. She will reject offerings of all other flowers, as it was when her daughter, Persephone, was out picking them that she was taken to the Underworld.

JANUARY/FEBRUARY

MONDAY (JANUARY)   29

TUESDAY (JANUARY)   30

WEDNESDAY (JANUARY)   31

THURSDAY FIRST DAY OF BLACK HISTORY MONTH   1

FRIDAY GROUNDHOG DAY (US / CAN)   2

SATURDAY   3

SUNDAY   4

FEBRUARY 2024

MONDAY 5

TUESDAY WAITANGI DAY OBSERVED (NZ) 6

WEDNESDAY 7

THURSDAY 8

FRIDAY ● ✦ **9**

SATURDAY CHINESE NEW YEAR **10**

SUNDAY **11**

An orchid's beauty must be seen—its
gift too rare to hide.
With orchid placed upon my wrist
I gain a sense of pride.

FEBRUARY 2024

MONDAY 12

TUESDAY 13

WEDNESDAY VALENTINE'S DAY / ASH WEDNESDAY 14

THURSDAY 15

FRIDAY 16

SATURDAY 17

SUNDAY 18

I open my heart to love. I am love.
I am loved. I am loving.
I love myself for all that I am
and all that I do.

FEBRUARY 2024

MONDAY PRESIDENTS' DAY (US)   **19**

TUESDAY   **20**

WEDNESDAY   **21**

THURSDAY   **22**

FRIDAY   **23**

SATURDAY ○   **24**

SUNDAY   **25**

Caraway's lore lies in preventing departure, thus its use in love potions and protecting items from being stolen.

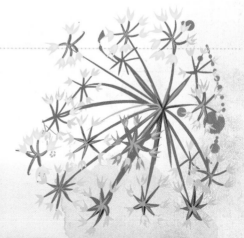

MARIGOLD | *Calendula officinalis*

PLANETARY COMPANION	DAILY CORRESPONDENCE
SUN	SUNDAY
ZODIAC SIGNS	ELEMENT
LEO, SAGITTARIUS	FIRE
ENERGY	
MASCULINE	

With a color as bright as the sunshine that teases them from the Earth, marigolds are sturdy and steadfast. They speak of grief when used with the language of flowers; a happier translation says marigolds mean "thinking of you," joy, and remembrance. Their petals taste slightly bitter and can be used like saffron threads or added to salads, if grown properly for culinary use.

MAGICAL PROPERTIES

Viewed as a cure-all, marigolds can protect your property from evil influences and help protect your garden from pests. They can influence legal matters, induce prophetic dreams, and increase your attraction to another. They also portend grace. If you concentrate, marigolds may also help you see those garden fairies taking shelter under their curly petals. Its association with the Sun arose from its habit of blooming in the morning.

SUGGESTED USE

Sprinkle marigolds under your bed to induce dreams to help you see into the future. Brighten a lapel with a marigold to attract good outcomes in legal matters, or place a lovely pot of marigolds outside your door to repel enemies from entering. Float marigold blossoms in your bath and emerge filled with an energy no one can resist.

O' sunny marigold, do shine your luck on me this day,
that judgment due at any time is rendered such my way.

INNER GODDESS STRENGTH

Summon your inner goddess strength and sit with any goddess of healing that resonates with you. Airmid is a favorite for her vast herbal healing knowledge and compassion.

Gather a black candle for protection or a green candle to channel the herbs Airmid works with, an amethyst or clear quartz crystal for its healing energies, and any healing herbs you can, such as angelica, bay leaf, fennel, ivy, lemon balm, or marigold. Essential oils can stand in—try chamomile, lavender, rose, sandalwood, or peppermint.

1. Anoint the candle with essential oil. Light the candle.

2. Muddle or crush the fresh herbs in your cauldron, if you have one, to release their healing oils, aromas, and energies.

3. Take a deep breath in and hold it, letting the herbal energies and the life-sustaining oxygen reach deep throughout your body. Exhale slowly.

4. Continue to breathe this way. When ready, say quietly or aloud:

That which heals can also harm,

respect I must these herbal balms.

With thoughts attuned to easing pain,

I pray your healing hands to lay

upon my [area to be healed],

draw ills away and speed release, to mend I may.

MARCH 2024

NOTES	SUNDAY	MONDAY	TUESDAY
	◗ 3	4	5
	● 10	11	12
	RAMADAN (BEGINS AT SUNDOWN) MOTHERING SUNDAY (UK)	LABOUR DAY (AUS-VIC)	
	◗ 17	18	19
	ST. PATRICK'S DAY		SPRING EQUINOX
	24	○ 25	26
	PALM SUNDAY		
	31		
	EASTER		

MARCH 2024

WEDNESDAY	THURSDAY	FRIDAY	SATURDAY
		1 FIRST DAY OF WOMEN'S HISTORY MONTH	2
6	7	8	9
13	14	15	16
20 NOWRUZ	21	22	23 PURIM (BEGINS AT SUNDOWN)
27	28	29 GOOD FRIDAY	30

TREE MAGIC TIPS

Trees can be powerful allies in your magical work. Get to know the souls of the trees native to your area—take a walk in your neighborhood or a park. Research various trees online. When you're drawn to a particular tree, it may be because its strength recognizes where you need attention.

- Leave an offering for the tree, representing your intentions, and ask for its help manifesting them.

- Play music on a wooden instrument to honor the tree's rich history.

- Use a tree's offerings, such as fallen nuts, pinecones, leaves, twigs, fruit, or flowers, on your altar, in spellwork, and for goddess offerings.

- Visualize a tree's particular strength as you call upon it in meditation.

- Savor the fragrance of essential oils, such as cedar, eucalyptus, fir, frankincense, orange, pine, and sandalwood, for their grounding, calming, nurturing, and recharging qualities.

FEBRUARY/MARCH

MONDAY (FEBRUARY) 26

TUESDAY (FEBRUARY) 27

WEDNESDAY (FEBRUARY) 28

THURSDAY (FEBRUARY) 29

FRIDAY FIRST DAY OF WOMEN'S HISTORY MONTH 1

SATURDAY 2

SUNDAY 3

MARCH 2024

MONDAY   4

TUESDAY   5

WEDNESDAY   6

THURSDAY   7

FRIDAY 8

SATURDAY 9

SUNDAY RAMADAN (BEGINS AT SUNDOWN) / MOTHERING SUNDAY (UK) 10

When melancholy strikes,
blue borage I do seek.
For borage blooms can lift the
cloud, return me to my peak.

MARCH 2024

MONDAY LABOUR DAY (AUS-VIC) 11

TUESDAY 12

WEDNESDAY 13

THURSDAY 14

FRIDAY 15

SATURDAY 16

SUNDAY ST. PATRICK'S DAY 17

*I place this birch broom by my door
to sweep away the dust and more.*

MONDAY 18

TUESDAY SPRING EQUINOX 19

WEDNESDAY NOWRUZ 20

THURSDAY 21

FRIDAY 22

SATURDAY PURIM (BEGINS AT SUNDOWN) 23

SUNDAY PALM SUNDAY 24

While reaching limbs to Sun-filled
skies and welcoming the rain,
abundant harvest, lush and strong,
each herb sings its refrain.

MARCH 2024

MONDAY ○   25

TUESDAY   26

WEDNESDAY   27

THURSDAY   28

FRIDAY GOOD FRIDAY

29

SATURDAY

30

SUNDAY EASTER

31

*Sunny flower, "tooth of lion," infuse
in me the strength of iron.*

FERN | *Pteridophyta* (division)

PLANETARY COMPANION	DAILY CORRESPONDENCE
MERCURY	WEDNESDAY
ZODIAC SIGN	ELEMENT
CAPRICORN	AIR
ENERGY	
MASCULINE	

A diverse group of plants numbering about twenty thousand species, ferns are at once prehistoric and soothing, fantastical and fairy-like. Fern tells tales of fascination. Because of its (then) mysterious propagation—fern produces neither flower nor seed—it was deduced that the seeds of a fern must be invisible. Legend tells that anyone carrying fern seeds in their pocket will also be invisible! And (logically?) that invisible seed must be born of the invisible flower, which is said to bloom but once a year at midnight on the summer solstice. Should you be lucky enough to spy said flower, you will be happy and rich for eternity.

MAGICAL PROPERTIES
Fern is known to boost the energy of other magical herbs, provide protection from evil witches, and improve mental clarity.

SUGGESTED USE
Boston ferns are known to detoxify the air. Keep one in your home anywhere a little fresh air—and sense of security—will help you breathe easier. Include ferns in any bouquets to amplify the message intended. Use in spells calling for protection from unseen evil. Grow for their soothing visual qualities. Use a frond to sprinkle Moon water on your altar to boost protective spells.

*O' fairest fern, I call on you to spread your fairy wings
to keep me safe from evil spells and other harmful things.*

INTUITION BOOST

The Waxing Moon's vibrational energy can heighten your natural intuition. Whether your intuition needs a boost from a slump or you need reassurance that you can trust what your intuition is telling you, try this spell.

Standing or sitting quietly, close your eyes. Let your mind be still, and listen to what you heart is telling you. Unsure what that is? Say quietly or aloud:

Cleansing Moon, cast your light—dispense the shadows nigh.

I call on you to heed my cry, awaken sights within.

Power my internal eye, make clear what I deny.

APRIL 2024

NOTES	SUNDAY	MONDAY	TUESDAY
		1 ☽ APRIL FOOLS' DAY	2
	7	8 ●	9 EID AL-FITR (BEGINS AT SUNDOWN)
	14	15 ☾	16
	21	22 PASSOVER (BEGINS AT SUNDOWN) EARTH DAY	23 ○
	28	29	30

APRIL 2024

WEDNESDAY	THURSDAY	FRIDAY	SATURDAY
3	4	5	6
10	11	12	13
17	18	19	20
24 ADMINISTRATIVE PROFESSIONALS' DAY (US)	25 ANZAC DAY (AUS / NZ)	26	27

HERBAL MAGIC CODES

Eye of newt and toe of frog, wool of bat and tongue of dog . . . This is likely one of the best-known examples of a witching spell, thanks to William Shakespeare's *Macbeth*, but where exactly did the three weird sisters source these unusual ingredients for their magical brew? You may be surprised to learn that, like any honored secret family recipe, early practitioners of herbal magic used secret code to protect their recipes and proprietary ingredients from pilfering by competitors. Thus, no animals were actually harmed in the creation of these spells.

Others include:

- Blood of goose: mulberry tree sap
- Bloody fingers: foxglove
- Ear of donkey: comfrey
- Horse's hoof: coltsfoot
- Lamb's ears: betony
- Swine's snout: dandelion leaves
- Bat's wing: holly leaves
- Elf leaf: lavender

APRIL

MONDAY APRIL FOOLS' DAY $\quad$ 1

TUESDAY $\quad$ 2

WEDNESDAY $\quad$ 3

THURSDAY $\quad$ 4

FRIDAY $\quad$ 5

SATURDAY $\quad$ 6

SUNDAY $\quad$ 7

APRIL 2024

MONDAY ● 8

TUESDAY EID AL-FITR (BEGINS AT SUNDOWN) 9

WEDNESDAY 10

THURSDAY 11

FRIDAY 12

SATURDAY 13

SUNDAY 14

A healthy herbal harvest is all but guaranteed as I scatter apple blossoms as far as I can see.

APRIL 2024

MONDAY 15

TUESDAY 16

WEDNESDAY 17

THURSDAY 18

FRIDAY

19

SATURDAY

20

SUNDAY

21

*I plant rosemary in remembrance—that
we never forget.*

APRIL 2024

MONDAY PASSOVER (BEGINS AT SUNDOWN) / EARTH DAY   **22**

TUESDAY ○   **23**

WEDNESDAY ADMINISTRATIVE PROFESSIONALS' DAY (US)   **24**

THURSDAY ANZAC DAY (AUS / NZ)   **25**

FRIDAY   26

SATURDAY   27

SUNDAY   28

Oak trees are shelter to many animals
and plants, notably mistletoe, the
esteemed magical plant of the Druids.

LEMON BALM | *Melissa officinalis*

PLANETARY COMPANIONS	DAILY CORRESPONDENCE
VENUS, MOON	MONDAY
ZODIAC SIGNS	ELEMENT
CANCER, GEMINI	WATER
ENERGY	
FEMININE	

Smelling sweetly of grass and lemon, this steady herb thrives most anywhere it's planted, setting roots that spread and establishing friends and family easily, of which lemon balm speaks fondly. Its stubborn optimism is hard to ignore; its comforting words a friend.

MAGICAL PROPERTIES
History tells us that lemon balm was used to keep the sacred honeybees cultivated at the Temple of Artemis happy and returning home. Choose lemon balm when family harmony is needed and friends and family need tending. It can ward away evil as well, ushering in health and love. Its gentle fragrance boosts memory and spirits.

SUGGESTED USE
Lemon balm's scent is instantly uplifting and cheerful. Add a bruised sprig to iced tea and inhale a sunny disposition as you savor the tea to soothe away any tension. Use an infusion to clean any room in the home that needs to be cleared of negative energy, such as after an illness, argument, or other negative experience. A joyful spirit will return. Sprinkle on a salad to entice a lover. To soothe a troubled spirit, hang a few sprigs, especially those just about to flower, on a mirror. Gaze into the mirror, honoring your innate goddess, and say quietly or aloud:

O' sacred herb, release in me your sweet uplifting joy,
to ease my fears and calm my tears and wash them from my eyes.

ANGER ANTIDOTE

When anger threatens to take you and your relationship under, stop, take a deep breath, and seek solace in an herbal charm.

- Lavender calms, chamomile murmurs soothing scents, and lemon balm clears the mind.

- Add Chinese chrysanthemum for cheerfulness in adversity, and Damask rose to refresh your thoughts of self-love.

Make a sachet to carry for unexpected events, or mindfully gather what you can from your garden as you seek to calm the mind. Create an herbal circle around a blue candle. Light the flame and gaze into it until you feel your heartbeat slow. Sip a soothing cup of chrysanthemum tea. Repeat the following as needed:

Sweet herbs and blooms whose charms doth soothe,

engage me in debate, for anger's rising fast

inside and tempting me to hate.

Do fill me with your calming voice to take up anger's place.

MAY 2024

NOTES	SUNDAY	MONDAY	TUESDAY
	5	**6**	**7**
	CINCO DE MAYO ORTHODOX EASTER	LABOUR DAY (AUS-QLD) EARLY MAY BANK HOLIDAY (UK)	
	12	**13**	**14**
	MOTHER'S DAY (US / CAN)		
	19	**20**	**21**
		VICTORIA DAY (CAN)	
	26	**27**	**28**
		SPRING BANK HOLIDAY (UK) MEMORIAL DAY (US)	

MAY 2024

WEDNESDAY	THURSDAY	FRIDAY	SATURDAY
1 FIRST DAY OF ASIAN AMERICAN AND PACIFIC ISLANDER HERITAGE MONTH	2	3	4 YOM HASHOAH (BEGINS AT SUNDOWN)
8	9	10	11
15	16	17	18
22 23		24	25
29 30		31	

PERSEPHONE/PROSERPINA

Persephone, wife of Hades, was the Greek goddess of vegetation, particularly grain. Her symbolism is that of the return of spring, as she was allowed back to Earth, from Hades, once a year, when the world burst again into bloom. When the need for rejuvenation or rebirth is of import, call on Persephone, who is especially fond of floral wreaths woven of spring flowers, crocus, daffodils, lilies, ivy, maidenhair fern, daisy, lavender, and pomegranate. Scatter these offerings along with your intentions and watch them grow.

APRIL / MAY

MONDAY (APRIL) 29

TUESDAY (APRIL) 30

WEDNESDAY FIRST DAY OF ASIAN AMERICAN AND PACIFIC ISLANDER HERITAGE MONTH 1

THURSDAY 2

FRIDAY 3

SATURDAY YOM HASHOAH (BEGINS AT SUNDOWN) 4

SUNDAY CINCO DE MAYO / ORTHODOX EASTER 5

MAY 2024

MONDAY LABOUR DAY (AUS-QLD) / EARLY MAY BANK HOLIDAY (UK)   **6**

TUESDAY   **7**

WEDNESDAY   **8**

THURSDAY   **9**

FRIDAY 10

SATURDAY 11

SUNDAY MOTHER'S DAY (US / CAN) 12

Let's toast to fortunes great and small,
may either come my way.
Refresh my glass, refill my hopes,
success is here to stay.

MAY 2024

MONDAY   13

TUESDAY   14

WEDNESDAY   15

THURSDAY   16

FRIDAY 17

SATURDAY 18

SUNDAY 19

Respect the Earth and the offerings she provides for your magical pursuits.

MAY 2024

MONDAY VICTORIA DAY (CAN)   **20**

TUESDAY   **21**

WEDNESDAY   **22**

THURSDAY ○   **23**

FRIDAY 24

SATURDAY 25

SUNDAY 26

With wave of their leaves
I restore peace and ease
that life does repair, heal, and flourish.

TANSY | *Tanacetum vulgare*

PLANETARY COMPANION
VENUS

DAILY CORRESPONDENCE
FRIDAY

ZODIAC SIGN
LEO

ELEMENT
WATER

ENERGY
FEMININE

Tansy's protective properties can speak aggressively toward others, but sometimes we must look after ourselves and set boundaries for protection. Tansy also offers thanks and gratitude in recognition of blessings. Tansy's record of use goes back to the ancient Greeks, and it was an herb grown in Charlemagne's garden. As Zeus's favorite, Ganymede was made immortal when given tansy. It was used ceremonially, medicinally, and in practical ways, like repelling mice and other vermin and varmints from the home. Tansy was also used for embalming, which, in addition to the legend of Ganymede, may relate to its association with immortality. Do not take tansy internally.

MAGICAL PROPERTIES
Tansy brings luck and offers protection from and reversal of any spells cast your way, thus promoting both luck and a good, long life.

SUGGESTED USE
Use tansy in protective spells and for a prosperous life. Place on your altar when work on setting boundaries is needed. Practically, planting tansy deters ants, but cut the flowers off before it goes to seed if you don't want tansy to become the pest.

Each day goes faster than the other;
I'd like to live to be one hundred.
With tansy planted by my door,
may health hold fast and my years be more.

BID EVIL SPIRITS ADIEU

Doors and windows are prime entry spots for evil to lurk. Keep entryways and windows clean and clear by sprinkling a little Himalayan salt in each of their corners, place tansy on your altar, and let sit for twenty-four hours to absorb negative energies. Imagine a white, cleansing light filtering the space as you sweep or vacuum any potential harm away. Once complete, take three deep breaths, exhaling from your mouth before saying quietly or aloud:

This home is blessed by light of day

and charmed by dark of night.

Where love abounds no evil is found

nor harmful agents fright.

JUNE 2024

NOTES	SUNDAY	MONDAY	TUESDAY
	2	3	4
	9	10	11
	16	17	18
	FATHER'S DAY (US / CAN / UK) 23	24	25
	30		

JUNE 2024

WEDNESDAY	THURSDAY	FRIDAY	SATURDAY
			1 FIRST DAY OF PRIDE MONTH
5 ●	6	7	8
12	13 ◐	14 FLAG DAY (US)	15
19 JUNETEENTH (US)	20 ○ SUMMER SOLSTICE	21	22
26	27 ◑	28	29

THE MOON AND HERBAL MAGIC

Pairing herbs with the Moon's energetic phases can add powerful and mindful influences to your work. Get ready to search the skies for a bit of cosmic correspondence—and, remember, even the smallest of signs can bear great meaning. And, as with all magic, time, patience, and practice are keys to the results you desire.

THE MOON'S GUIDING FORCES
It takes about twenty-nine days for the Moon to pass through all eight phases. The Moon's phases offer a cycle of light and dark times—quiet, rest, and contemplation. Understanding the energies and rhythms of the Universe to help bring about our intentions.

THE MOON'S GUIDING PHASES
Use the waxing (growing) and waning (diminishing) energies of the Moon's changing phases to set, implement, evaluate and revise, achieve, celebrate, and assess your intention-filled life. Coordinating your herbal allies, thoughts, dreams, and plans with the Moon's natural cycle can help you achieve all you hope for. Nurture, tend, and grow your dreams as the phases unfold. The magic is there for the taking.

MAY / JUNE

MONDAY (MAY) SPRING BANK HOLIDAY (UK) / MEMORIAL DAY (US)   **27**

TUESDAY (MAY)   **28**

WEDNESDAY (MAY)   **29**

THURSDAY (MAY)   **30**

FRIDAY (MAY)   **31**

SATURDAY FIRST DAY OF PRIDE MONTH   **1**

SUNDAY   **2**

JUNE 2024

MONDAY 3

TUESDAY 4

WEDNESDAY 5

THURSDAY 6

FRIDAY 7

SATURDAY 8

SUNDAY 9

When the scent from these herbs fade,
they've filled my heart with bliss.

JUNE 2024

MONDAY 10

TUESDAY 11

WEDNESDAY 12

THURSDAY 13

FRIDAY FLAG DAY (US) 14

SATURDAY 15

SUNDAY FATHER'S DAY (US / CAN / UK) 16

Aloe gel, join this spell, reach deep within your curing well of healing balm and soothing calm that everything will soon be well.

JUNE 2024

MONDAY 17

TUESDAY 18

WEDNESDAY JUNETEENTH (US) 19

THURSDAY SUMMER SOLSTICE 20

FRIDAY ○   **21**

SATURDAY   **22**

SUNDAY   **23**

An angel's kiss has blessed this herb,
as Nature's story tells,
an angel's grace is sought this day,
protective, true, and bold.

JUNE 2024

MONDAY 24

TUESDAY 25

WEDNESDAY 26

THURSDAY 27

FRIDAY ◗ 28

SATURDAY 29

SUNDAY 30

The willow's flexibility reminds us to bend with the winds to weather life's storms.

YARROW | *Achillea millefolium*

PLANETARY COMPANIONS
MARS, VENUS

DAILY CORRESPONDENCES
TUESDAY, FRIDAY

ZODIAC SIGNS
ARIES, PISCES, GEMINI, LIBRA, TAURUS

ELEMENT
WATER

ENERGY
FEMININE

This ancient plant companion has been found in Neanderthal burial sites along with chamomile. In the language of herbs, yarrow can soothe an aching heart. Yarrow's Latin name, *Achillea*, comes from the great warrior Achilles, who is said to have used the herb to heal the wounds of his soldiers. Because of its great healing properties, this herb has been used medicinally throughout the ages and by various cultures. With its bitter scent, yarrow has even been used as an ingredient to brew beer.

MAGICAL PROPERTIES
Yarrow is strongest when used in healing spells. It can also heighten intuitive abilities to divine one's true love.

SUGGESTED USE
Use yarrow in any love spells, especially when identifying your true love is of concern. Include yarrow in wedding flowers to ensure at least seven years of a happy marriage. Keep it on your person (sachet, charm bag, wear it) for a strong personal protective energy. If pregnant, hold yarrow on your right side to ensure an easy labor. Stuff yarrow into dream pillows to promote prophetic dreams.

I wish to know now my betrothed, please yarrow tell me who.
I wear your blossoms on my heart that they reveal somehow
the one who's meant to marry me, I'll pledge my whole troth to.

WISHES AND DREAMS JAR

Whether wishing for that new person in your life or dreaming of your future with the one you already have, a wishes and dreams jar can capture the magic and preserve it to multiply. Alter the herbs, flowers, and crystals based on the energy or wish that you seek to attract to you.

Select a Mason jar with a lid, as large or as small as you like. Gather these herbs:

- Basil for luck and love
- Lemon balm for compassion
- Dill for good cheer
- Oregano for joy
- Sage for wisdom
- Yarrow for courage and everlasting love

Place your items in a basket and infuse them overnight with the power of the New Moon to set your intentions. Then, place the items in your jar, seal it, and place it on your altar to be reminded of your wishes and dreams. When passing by, take a moment to reflect on your desires and say quietly or aloud:

Sweet herbs, do work for me, with all emotions

so bestowed when life doth take the bumpy road

I know my heart will still be true

and love grows then beyond what's new.

JULY 2024

NOTES	SUNDAY	MONDAY	TUESDAY
		1 CANADA DAY (CAN)	2
	7	8	9
	14	15	16
	○ 21	22	23
	28	29	30

JULY 2024

WEDNESDAY	THURSDAY	FRIDAY	SATURDAY
3	4	5	6
	INDEPENDENCE DAY (US)		
10	11	12	13
17	18	19	20
24	25	26	27
31			

CELEBRATING DIFFERENCES

The thrilling diversity of the herbal kingdom is something we celebrate and yearn to learn more about, and so it should be with the uplifting diversity of the human kingdom. When differences threaten to divide instead of delight, learning more about them is the first step to understanding differences aren't always as different as they first appear.

Gather cinquefoil, mugwort, sage, and willow for wisdom; morning glory and rosemary for acceptance; sweet pea for friendship; and nasturtium for working in harmony. Invite the wisdom of your favorite goddess in for a chat. When ready to seek common ground, say quietly or aloud:

These herbs in friendship offered are, with purest of intent

to let the conversation flow, to understand what's meant

by words and deeds, to sow the seeds of wisdom

and accept what's different.

JULY

MONDAY CANADA DAY (CAN) — **1**

TUESDAY — **2**

WEDNESDAY — **3**

THURSDAY INDEPENDENCE DAY (US) — **4**

FRIDAY 🌑 — **5**

SATURDAY — **6**

SUNDAY — **7**

JULY 2024

MONDAY   8

TUESDAY   9

WEDNESDAY   10

THURSDAY   11

FRIDAY 12

SATURDAY 13

SUNDAY 14

With caraway I bless this house
that it becomes a home where
love and faith and trust abound and
fear does never roam.

JULY 2024

MONDAY   15

TUESDAY   16

WEDNESDAY   17

THURSDAY   18

FRIDAY   19

SATURDAY   20

SUNDAY ○   21

*I ask the Sun and Moon to bless
these seeds I wish to grow.
To warm and coax, encourage, and
feed to spread their roots below.*

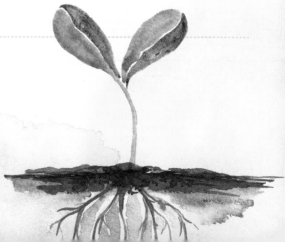

JULY 2024

MONDAY 22

TUESDAY 23

WEDNESDAY 24

THURSDAY 25

FRIDAY 26

SATURDAY 27

SUNDAY 28

*A circle drawn with a hazel branch is
said to afford instant protection, and
garden fairies find the nuts delightful.*

CHAMOMILE | *Matricaria recutita*
| *Chamaemelum nobile*

PLANETARY COMPANIONS
SUN, MOON

DAILY CORRESPONDENCES
SUNDAY, MONDAY

ZODIAC SIGNS
AQUARIUS, LEO

ELEMENT
WATER

ENERGY
MASCULINE

Chamomile's soothing words speak of patience in hard times. This herb has a long history of use in folk, medicinal, and cultural practices. The two most common types, Roman and German chamomile, are similar plants, easily confused, and interchangeable. Their main differences lie in their growth habits and life span. It is said one must bow before the plant in honor of its healing power. Several cultures believed bathing newborns in chamomile water enchanted, purified, and blessed the baby. Its white blossom channels purity.

MAGICAL PROPERTIES
Among its many charms, chamomile can conjure sleep, purification, love, money, evil eye protection, and strength in difficult times.

SUGGESTED USE
Give a bouquet to express admiration for someone's courage and to bolster their spirits. Drink an infusion to foster positivity and cultivate inner calm and focus. Add to sleep pillows for inducing sleep and prophetic dreams. Use chamomile branches to sprinkle chamomile water anywhere cleansing or blessing is needed. Use in any love, healing, prosperity, work, or home and family spells.

I've brewed intent into this tea—a double wish to bring,
for fortune's gone and left me dry, with life more challenging.
With every sip, I thank you for your truly magic way,
whose luck I reap that feels a heap like I grabbed the golden ring.

LOKAHI HARMONIOUS HOME

In Indigenous Hawaiian healing practices, the word "lokahi" represents harmony with the world and people around you. The "Lokahi Triangle" speaks to physical, mental, and spiritual balance. To honor the sacred number 3, and to invite that balance, all ingredients included in this spell should be added in 3s: 3 pinches, 3 drops.

In a sachet pouch, intentionally add:

- Chamomile for serenity and calm
- Garden sage for purification
- Bay leaf with your intention written on it
- 3 drops lavender essential oil
- 3 drops peppermint essential oil

Once completed, tie the sachet closed and place it hidden in any part of your home that has been feeling unharmonious or tense.

AUGUST 2024

NOTES	SUNDAY	MONDAY	TUESDAY
	● 4	5	6
		SUMMER BANK HOLIDAY (UK-SCT)	
	11	◑ 12	13
	18	○ 19	20
	25	◐ 26	27
		SUMMER BANK HOLIDAY (UK-ENG / NIR / WAL)	

AUGUST 2024

WEDNESDAY	THURSDAY	FRIDAY	SATURDAY
	1	2	3
7	8	9	10
14	15	16	17
21	22	23	24
28	29	30	31

PLANETARY COMPANIONS

Just as we can see the influence of the Moon's phases on tides across the Earth, or the Sun's ability to evaporate raindrops and initiate growth, each herb has a classical planetary companion that lends its powerful status and wisdom to the herb's own power.

DAILY CORRESPONDENCES

As the days of the week are named for the planets, crafting a spell, ritual, or prayer on a particular day triples the energetic influence of the herbs being used (planetary influence + daily influence + herbal energies).

- Sunday for the Sun
- Monday for the Moon
- Tuesday for Mars
- Wednesday for Mercury
- Thursday for Jupiter
- Friday for Venus
- Saturday for Saturn

JULY/AUGUST

MONDAY (JULY)   29

TUESDAY (JULY)   30

WEDNESDAY (JULY)   31

THURSDAY   1

FRIDAY   2

SATURDAY   3

SUNDAY ●   4

AUGUST 2024

MONDAY SUMMER BANK HOLIDAY (UK-SCT) | 5

TUESDAY | 6

WEDNESDAY | 7

THURSDAY | 8

FRIDAY 9

SATURDAY 10

SUNDAY 11

These herbs all from the
Earth I've plucked,
to sprinkle dreams with fertile luck.

AUGUST 2024

MONDAY ☽   12

TUESDAY   13

WEDNESDAY   14

THURSDAY   15

FRIDAY 16

SATURDAY 17

SUNDAY 18

*With bay in hand I proudly stand
before the goddess realm
for glory to the sisterhood of
those who came before.*

AUGUST 2024

MONDAY ○ 19

TUESDAY 20

WEDNESDAY 21

THURSDAY 22

FRIDAY 23

SATURDAY 24

SUNDAY 25

A dash of pepper starts the spell;
a sprinkle keeps me safe
from evil eyes and other harms that
do invade my space.

GINSENG (KOREAN) | *Panax ginseng*

PLANETARY COMPANION	DAILY CORRESPONDENCE
SUN	SUNDAY
ZODIAC SIGN	ELEMENT
SCORPIO	FIRE
ENERGY	
MASCULINE	

This mystical plant has been around for thousands of years. The phrase "money talks" applies mightily to ginseng, such is its demand, especially in China, where it has been long revered for its medicinal properties. However, at a growth rate that provides harvestable roots in about seven years—and the longer they grow, the more valuable they become—Korean ginseng is not a quick-to-market product. As such, American ginseng, *Panax quinquefolius*, which grows more quickly, is threatened due to overharvesting.

MAGICAL PROPERTIES
Ginseng traditionally promotes longevity, health, beauty, and vitality. It is also said to stimulate lust and sexual prowess due to this root's, sometimes, quite humanlike shape.

SUGGESTED USE
Include ginseng root in all your love charms for satisfactory results. Burn ginseng to remove evil elements from a home. Create a protective ginseng spray: Soak ginseng root in water for 3 days, then place the bowl of water under the Moon's energizing light for 1 night (the Full Moon is best). Transfer the water to a spray bottle and use it to clean your home, spritz your altar to purify it, or spritz yourself for its protective charms (keep the spritz away from your face).

As ginseng root grows long and deep, its age enhances charm.
I call on ginseng's mystic lore to keep me safe from harm
that long this life of mine may be, its memories to warm.

HOMELY WISHES

When wishing, dreaming, pining for a place to call home, a little herbal magic for luck can't be a bad idea. Fire up your cauldron and "cook" a nice herbal stew as a housewarming present to yourself.

In your cauldron, combine as many of the following as you can. As you add each ingredient to season your wish for a new home, picture what that home looks like and how you will feel living in it.

- For wishes granted: ginseng
- For home: chamomile
- For hearth goddess wisdom: call on Hestia
- For new beginnings: birch
- For a little luck: nutmeg
- For protection: mistletoe

SEPTEMBER 2024

NOTES	SUNDAY	MONDAY	TUESDAY
	1 FATHER'S DAY (AUS / NZ)	2 LABOR DAY (US) LABOUR DAY (CAN)	3
	8 GRANDPARENTS' DAY (US)	9	10
	15 FIRST DAY OF NATIONAL HISPANIC HERITAGE MONTH	16 ○	17
	22 FALL EQUINOX	23 ☽	24
	29	30	

SEPTEMBER 2024

WEDNESDAY	THURSDAY	FRIDAY	SATURDAY
4	5	6	7
11	12	13	14
PATRIOT DAY (US)			
18	19	20	21
25	26	27	28

A LITTLE KITCHEN MAGIC

Turn your kitchen into a magical dispensary and your herbal spell jars into edible gifts to spread a little magic around. Create a custom label to convey the message and fill the jars with your own special type of magic. Some ideas to get you started:

- Apple butter for family harmony and love; conjure the spirit of the goddesses Demeter, Freya, and Gaia, or good wishes for fame.

- Custom tea blends for a variety of wishes and dreams.

- Herbal-flavored sea salts, such as with dried rosemary for remembrance for a special friend; or thyme for beauty, protection, happiness, and good health; or a combination of rosemary, thyme, sage, and lavender for their magical properties.

AUGUST/SEPTEMBER

MONDAY (AUGUST) SUMMER BANK HOLIDAY (UK-ENG / NIR / WAL) ◗   26

TUESDAY (AUGUST)   27

WEDNESDAY (AUGUST)   28

THURSDAY (AUGUST)   29

FRIDAY (AUGUST)   30

SATURDAY (AUGUST)   31

SUNDAY FATHER'S DAY (AUS / NZ)   1

SEPTEMBER 2024

MONDAY LABOR DAY (US) / LABOUR DAY (CAN) ● 2

TUESDAY 3

WEDNESDAY 4

THURSDAY 5

FRIDAY 6

SATURDAY 7

SUNDAY GRANDPARENTS' DAY (US) 8

I bless these seven cloves
with friendship deep and true
and call on love's great power
that the message reaches you.

SEPTEMBER 2024

MONDAY

9

TUESDAY

10

WEDNESDAY PATRIOT DAY (US)

11

THURSDAY

12

FRIDAY 13

SATURDAY 14

SUNDAY FIRST DAY OF NATIONAL HISPANIC HERITAGE MONTH 15

Cardamom instills faithful love, lures lust, and brings on a sweetness of temperament.

SEPTEMBER 2024

MONDAY

16

TUESDAY ○

17

WEDNESDAY

18

THURSDAY

19

FRIDAY 20

SATURDAY 21

SUNDAY FALL EQUINOX 22

*A journey calls and I must go, but
comfrey comes along
to keep the luck of travel smooth and
sailing winds blow strong.*

SEPTEMBER 2024

MONDAY 23

TUESDAY 24

WEDNESDAY 25

THURSDAY 26

FRIDAY 27

SATURDAY 28

SUNDAY 29

So drunk in love I wish to be, I sip this catnip and rose tea.

TEA, BLACK | *Camellia sinensis*

PLANETARY COMPANIONS	DAILY CORRESPONDENCES
SUN, MARS	SUNDAY, TUESDAY

ZODIAC SIGN	ELEMENT
SAGITTARIUS	FIRE

ENERGY	
MASCULINE	

For centuries, people have turned to a cup of tea to soothe the nerves and relax the spirit. Because it has caffeine, black tea is sometimes not "technically" considered an herb. But because it is a plant with a storied history of use, both ceremonially and commonly, in cultures throughout the world, it is included here. You decide, but why dismiss any magical potential without at least trying it? Even science is now beginning to understand how it truly does reduce stress levels. Interestingly, black, green, and white tea all come from the same plant. The difference is in their growing, harvesting, processing, and oxidation levels, with black tea having the highest level and white tea having the least.

MAGICAL PROPERTIES
Tea leaves tell of futures yet seen. They invite luck, instill faith, foster protection, and (perhaps related to their future-seeing properties) heighten intuition.

SUGGESTED USE
Burn leaves, or drink a brewed cup, to attract riches. Sip the perfect cup while meditating to prepare for ritual work. Brew your intentions into your tea, adding herbs, flowers, and other energies related to your intentions. Add to dream sachets for relaxing sleep or money sachets for some extra jingle in your pocket.

With patience I do steep and brew the heart of my intent in you
that empty cup may signal true great riches that are overdue.

BREATHE OUT STRESS

A little stress can be an inspiring motivator, but when the pressure builds and threatens to derail you, take a breather to regain your balance. Choose from these or others you prefer:

- Black tea
- Chamomile
- Ginger, to sip
- Lavender, to bathe
- Rosemary

Close your eyes and inhale the herbs' rejuvenating scents. Breathe out the stress of the moment. Repeat several times, taking deep mindful breaths. When ready, say quietly:

Your calming scents do ease my stress and soothe my cares away.

Your leaves relieve my thoughts that tease and tempt my sanity.

Your stems stand strong, to urge me on, to stand and face the fray.

OCTOBER 2024

NOTES	SUNDAY	MONDAY	TUESDAY
			1
	6	7 LABOUR DAY (AUS-ACT / NSW / SA)	8
	13	14 INDIGENOUS PEOPLES' DAY (US) COLUMBUS DAY (US) THANKSGIVING DAY (CAN)	15
	20	21	22
	27	28 LABOUR DAY (NZ)	29

OCTOBER 2024

WEDNESDAY	THURSDAY	FRIDAY	SATURDAY
● 2 ROSH HASHANAH (BEGINS AT SUNDOWN)	3	4	5
9	◐ 10	11 YOM KIPPUR (BEGINS AT SUNDOWN)	12
16	○ 17	18	19
SUKKOT (BEGINS AT SUNDOWN)			
23	◑ 24 SIMCHAT TORAH (BEGINS AT SUNDOWN)	25	26
30	31 FIRST DAY OF DIWALI HALLOWEEN		

A PERFECT CUPPA

Whether you want to use your teatime to correspond with a particular Moon phase for spellwork or to relax for a spell, the perfect cuppa is a powerful potion. To make the perfect cup of herbal tea, whether you choose to purchase dried or fresh herbs, or use herbs you've grown in your magical garden, always use organic for their purity.

A general formula is 2 to 3 teaspoons of dried herbs (weight varies) for each 8 ounces (240 ml) of boiling water. For larger quantities, say a 1-gallon (3.8 L) jar, start with about 1 cup (weight varies) of dried herbs. Some herbs are stronger than others, so experiment to find the perfect ratio for your tastes and the specific herbs, or combination of herbs, you enjoy.

SEPTEMBER / OCTOBER

MONDAY (SEPTEMBER) 30

TUESDAY 1

WEDNESDAY ROSH HASHANAH (BEGINS AT SUNDOWN) 2

THURSDAY 3

FRIDAY 4

SATURDAY 5

SUNDAY 6

OCTOBER 2024

MONDAY LABOUR DAY (AUS-ACT / NSW / SA)   7

TUESDAY   8

WEDNESDAY   9

THURSDAY   10

FRIDAY YOM KIPPUR (BEGINS AT SUNDOWN) 11

SATURDAY 12

SUNDAY 13

*Keep bleeding heart in sight
to remind you that no matter
the loss, love will bloom again.*

OCTOBER 2024

MONDAY INDIGENOUS PEOPLES' DAY (US) / COLUMBUS DAY (US) / THANKSGIVING DAY (CAN) 14

TUESDAY 15

WEDNESDAY SUKKOT (BEGINS AT SUNDOWN) 16

THURSDAY ○ 17

FRIDAY 18

SATURDAY 19

SUNDAY 20

*Sweet William's face is filled
with joy, a song of cheer,
a needed refrain.*

OCTOBER 2024

MONDAY 21

TUESDAY 22

WEDNESDAY 23

THURSDAY SIMCHAT TORAH (BEGINS AT SUNDOWN) 24

FRIDAY   25

SATURDAY   26

SUNDAY   27

With ginger tea, a spell, and me
combining into sacred three
but triple in intensity to manifest
my destiny.

TURMERIC | *Curcuma longa*

PLANETARY COMPANIONS	DAILY CORRESPONDENCES
SUN, JUPITER	SUNDAY, THURSDAY
ZODIAC SIGN	ELEMENT
CANCER	FIRE
ENERGY	
MASCULINE	

Golden turmeric's message is of health and healing, as well as ingenuity in making do with what's available. It has a long history of ritual use for purification. Turmeric also has a long and varied history by herbal medicine practitioners dating back four thousand years and many of its health claims are bearing true under recent scientific scrutiny, including its antioxidant, antimicrobial, and anti-inflammatory properties, as well as its potential use in cancer treatment. As a spice, turmeric is widely used in South Asian and Middle Eastern cooking. Due to its color, it's been called Indian saffron. It's also used cosmetically and in food production for its color.

MAGICAL PROPERTIES
Turmeric promotes and protects good health and offers protective and cleansing energies (though be careful, as this herb is also known for creating a brilliant yellow/orange dye that is not very cleansing when unwanted).

SUGGESTED USE
Cast a circle for protection (outside). Add to homemade chicken noodle soup to boost its natural healing energies when cold, flu, or pandemic season hits. Find a recipe for golden milk online, or add a dash of turmeric to ginger tea, and relax into its healing, warming goodness on a cold day. Include the root in a healing charm bag or poppet.

Of hale and hardy health am I and like so wish to stay—
like an apple a day, turmeric's spicy ways heal what ails like the
Sun's shining rays.

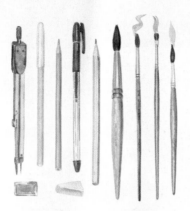

VISION BOARD SPELL

As with anything in life that we desire, it's essential to define our goals so that we can work actively toward them. This vision board is for when you don't have the words to express your desires, so you let your creativity take over. Make the message as clear as you can so that when you look at it, you'll instantly be reminded of your intentions.

If you have it, grab some turmeric from your spice cabinet and have a taste. Turmeric is a spice of creativity and energy. To begin your board, you'll need a canvas, either a poster board or cardstock will work. Gather pens, markers, or paints. Combine colors, make sigils, write your intentions—anything that gets your message across. Lastly, add the finishing touches with glitter glue, pictures, or washi tape stickers. Once you're done, place your board somewhere you're going to see it every day, so your intentions are clear, and you don't settle for less.

NOVEMBER 2024

NOTES	SUNDAY	MONDAY	TUESDAY
	3	4	5
			ELECTION DAY (US)
	10	11	12
		VETERANS DAY (US)	
	17	18	19
	24	25	26

NOVEMBER 2024

WEDNESDAY	THURSDAY	FRIDAY	SATURDAY
		1 ALL SAINTS' DAY	2
6	7	8	9
13	14	15	16
20	21	22	23
27	28 THANKSGIVING DAY (US)	29 NATIVE AMERICAN HERITAGE DAY (US)	30

ZODIAC SIGNS

Each Sun sign of the zodiac is known for certain traits embodied by those born under its influence. Knowing your sign and the signs of those you love, along with the sign's associated traits, can help you mix and match herbs, colors, elemental influences, days of the week, and even planetary powers to direct your herbal magic energies toward the positive and away from the negative.

The Sun sign for the end of October and most of November is Scorpio, represented by the scorpion (October 24 to November 22). A water sign, Scorpio's plants are hearty, persistent, and a little thorny. They speak of passion, bravery, and resiliency and their energies can be used to counter jealousy, secrecy, and emotional instability.

OCTOBER / NOVEMBER

MONDAY (OCTOBER) LABOUR DAY (NZ)   28

TUESDAY (OCTOBER)   29

WEDNESDAY (OCTOBER)   30

THURSDAY (OCTOBER) HALLOWEEN / FIRST DAY OF DIWALI   31

FRIDAY ALL SAINTS' DAY   1

SATURDAY   2

SUNDAY   3

NOVEMBER 2024

MONDAY 4

TUESDAY ELECTION DAY (US) 5

WEDNESDAY 6

THURSDAY 7

FRIDAY 8

SATURDAY ☽ 9

SUNDAY 10

*Of calming hue and soothing scent,
please, lavender, sing your song
to carry me to 'yon new day, restored,
renewed, and strong.*

NOVEMBER 2024

MONDAY VETERANS DAY (US)   **11**

TUESDAY   **12**

WEDNESDAY   **13**

THURSDAY   **14**

FRIDAY ◯ 15

SATURDAY 16

SUNDAY 17

Oregano—sprinkle my life with joy:
I've a sprig here for luck to employ.

NOVEMBER 2024

MONDAY 18

TUESDAY 19

WEDNESDAY 20

THURSDAY 21

FRIDAY **22**

SATURDAY **23**

SUNDAY **24**

*For ties that bind in love and life cannot
be yet undone. As time goes by it pulls
our hearts still closer, as if one.*

MISTLETOE | *Viscum album* *(Santalaceae family)*

| PLANETARY COMPANION | DAILY CORRESPONDENCE |
| SUN | SUNDAY |

| ZODIAC SIGN | ELEMENT |
| LIBRA | AIR |

| ENERGY | |
| MASCULINE | |

Revered as sacred by the Druids for its life-affirming abilities—especially when found growing on the sacred oak—this plant disregards the rules: It germinates in the dark and blooms in winter, in even the toughest conditions. The plant grows upside down—and sideways—or any which way it can, feeding off a host or supporting itself as it sees fit. Its evergreen leaves symbolize life. In the language of flowers, mistletoe signifies strength and the ability to surmount difficult odds. It is also thought to be strongly protective in its charms. Know your plants and be warned: This plant is poisonous, but popular, so be aware of where and how you use it.

MAGICAL PROPERTIES
Mistletoe fosters love, breeds fertility, provides protection, and is helpful in overcoming difficult circumstances.

SUGGESTED USE
A ring of mistletoe worn around the neck is said to provide a cloak of invisibility. Place it in the bedroom to encourage dreams. Hang it freely throughout your home to protect the love nurtured there and any children in the house; it can also attract luck and good fortune, stimulate fertility, and ward off evil spirits. Be forewarned that refusing a kiss under the mistletoe is said to bring bad luck—so don't play hard to get.

For fertile luck I turn to thee, dear mistletoe that blooms so free
in circumstance less than those designed to nurture plants like thee.
I strive for life to grow in me as evergreen and joyously,
to nurture life within my womb as mighty oak supports your bloom.

DIVINE WINTER PROTECTION

A divine fruit, oranges have delighted people long before they were as widely available as they are today. Once reserved as a special Christmastime treat in Europe, they helped to prevent scurvy in the long winter months. While we may not need them to ward off scurvy these days, they can still help us in warding off bad luck.

To clear your space of bad energy and call in good luck, boil two sliced oranges, one sliced lemon, two cinnamon sticks, a smattering of cloves, cranberries, and enough water to cover it all. Hang mistletoe under archways for added protection.

While preparing your home, say quietly or aloud:

With ample offering of fruit and spice

I bless this space free from vice.

Welcome are those who come to share

for with the support of each other

there is no storm for us to weather.

DECEMBER 2024

NOTES	SUNDAY	MONDAY	TUESDAY
	1 ● WORLD AIDS DAY	2	3 INTERNATIONAL DAY OF PERSONS WITH DISABILITIES
	8 ◖	9	10 HUMAN RIGHTS DAY
	15 ○	16	17
	22 ◗	23	24 CHRISTMAS EVE
	29	30 ●	31 NEW YEAR'S EVE

DECEMBER 2024

WEDNESDAY	THURSDAY	FRIDAY	SATURDAY
4	5	6	7
11	12	13	14
18	19	20	21 WINTER SOLSTICE
25 CHRISTMAS DAY HANUKKAH (BEGINS AT SUNDOWN)	26 BOXING DAY (UK / CAN / AUS / NZ) FIRST DAY OF KWANZAA	27	28

PROTECTIVE WREATH

Made from natural materials, such as herbs, twigs, flowers, and more, wreaths are more than decorative and have served many purposes throughout time. The wreath, an unending circle, symbolizes eternity and the cycle of the seasons. Hanging a wreath on your door can also be a symbol of protection for the home. Customize your wreath based on your intentions and take advantage of seasonal materials, such as herbs in your garden, to refresh and boost the energies you'd like to raise.

Use these protective herbs, dress up and protect your home with the energies of the seasons:

- Angelica
- Basil
- Bay laurel
- Dill
- Fern
- Foxglove
- Holly
- Mugwort
- Oak leaves and acorns
- Rosemary
- Rowan
- Sage
- Star anise
- Witch hazel

I cast this circle on my door; with herbs so rich and deep in lore,
that from all ills protected be,
my home will ne'er be harmed nor poor.

NOVEMBER / DECEMBER

MONDAY (NOVEMBER)   25

TUESDAY (NOVEMBER)   26

WEDNESDAY (NOVEMBER)   27

THURSDAY (NOVEMBER) THANKSGIVING DAY (US)   28

FRIDAY (NOVEMBER) NATIVE AMERICAN HERITAGE DAY (US)   29

SATURDAY (NOVEMBER)   30

SUNDAY WORLD AIDS DAY   1

DECEMBER 2024

MONDAY 2

TUESDAY INTERNATIONAL DAY OF PERSONS WITH DISABILITIES 3

WEDNESDAY 4

THURSDAY 5

FRIDAY

6

SATURDAY

7

SUNDAY

8

Beautiful rose, as your petals unfurl,
attract my heart's desire.
Delicate rose, as your beauty does grow,
may your charms unleashed inspire.

DECEMBER 2024

MONDAY 9

TUESDAY HUMAN RIGHTS DAY 10

WEDNESDAY 11

THURSDAY 12

FRIDAY

13

SATURDAY

14

SUNDAY ◯

15

With tarragon in hand, a
dragon-slayer I become
to conquer fears that keep me
from the life I need to own.

DECEMBER 2024

MONDAY   16

TUESDAY   17

WEDNESDAY   18

THURSDAY   19

FRIDAY 20

SATURDAY WINTER SOLSTICE 21

SUNDAY 22

Acorn, buckeye, honeysuckle, and
poppy bring luck and money.

DECEMBER 2024

MONDAY 23

TUESDAY CHRISTMAS EVE 24

WEDNESDAY CHRISTMAS DAY / HANUKKAH (BEGINS AT SUNDOWN) 25

THURSDAY BOXING DAY (UK / CAN / AUS / NZ) / FIRST DAY OF KWANZAA 26

FRIDAY   27

SATURDAY   28

SUNDAY   29

With powers ripe to stir new life—each
bloom, each leaf, and seed—
within the Earth to bloom again as
much as within me.

DECEMBER 2024

MONDAY ●   **30**

TUESDAY NEW YEAR'S EVE   **31**

WEDNESDAY (JANUARY) NEW YEAR'S DAY   **1**

THURSDAY (JANUARY)   **2**

NOTES

Notes

NOTES

NOTES

NOTES

The Quarto Group

Inspiring | Educating | Creating | Entertaining

Brimming with creative inspiration, how-to projects, and useful information to enrich your everyday life, quarto.com is a favorite destination for those pursuing their interests and passions.

© 2023 by Quarto Publishing Group USA Inc.

First published in 2023 by Rock Point,
an imprint of The Quarto Group,
142 West 36th Street, 4th Floor
New York, NY 10018, USA
T (212) 779-4972 F (212) 779-6058
www.Quarto.com

Contains content previously published in 2021 as *Herbal Magic* and in 2022 as *Love Spells*, *Moon Spells*, and *Protection Spells* by Wellfleet Press, an imprint of The Quarto Group, 142 West 36th Street, 4th Floor, New York, NY 10018

Rock Point titles are also available at discount for retail, wholesale, promotional, and bulk purchase.
For details, contact the Special Sales Manager by email at specialsales@quarto.com
or by mail at The Quarto Group, Attn: Special Sales Manager,
100 Cummings Center Suite 265D, Beverly, MA 01915 USA.

10 9 8 7 6 5 4 3 2 1

ISBN: 978-1-63106-952-9

Publisher: Rage Kindelsperger
Creative Director: Laura Drew
Managing Editor: Cara Donaldson
Editor: Sara Bonacum
Editorial Assistant: Katelynn Abraham
Interior Design: Laura Klynstra
Layout Design: Carlos Esparza

Printed in China

This planner provides general information on various widely known and widely accepted self-care practices. However, it should not be relied upon as recommending or promoting any specific diagnosis or method of treatment for a particular condition, and it is not intended as a substitute for medical advice or for direct diagnosis and treatment of a medical condition by a qualified physician. Readers who have questions about a particular condition, possible treatments for that condition, or possible reactions from the condition or its treatment should consult a physician or other qualified healthcare professional.

All Moon phases shown are for the Eastern Time Zone.